# From
# KING'S HEATH
## to the Country

### Volume 2

including Maypole, Yardley Wood
and Happy Valley

## More views from the past

## Barrie Geens

ISBN 978 0 9534775 8 6

Printed in Great Britain by
Amadeus Press, Cleckheaton

# –ACKNOWLEDGEMENTS–

I am grateful for the help that has been given to me in the preparation of this book by the following
people:

Alan Wycherley, Pat Sumner, Kate Keown, Michael Williams, Mark Norton, Brian Walsh, Stanley
Overton, Vernon and Hazel Fisher, Bob Chedgzoy, Patrick Hurley, The Lukeman family, Molly Budd,
Terry Pearson, Andy Bishop, Colin Baker, Mike Walsh, Jean Fenton, Viv Lawson, Joan Andrews,
Colin Scrivener, David Postle and to my wife, Sue for her continued support.

# CONTENTS

*Front Cover:* A 1950s post card view of Alcester Road South with Kings the drapers prominent and a number 11 Outer Circle bus about to turn into Vicarage Road.　　*Author's collection*

*Back Cover:* *Top* - A young railway porter awaits another arrival on the down platform c1906.
　　　　　　　　　　　　　　　　　　　　　*Author's collection*

*Bottom* - A peaceful scene by the cottages in Slade Lane, looking towards the River Cole crossing.　This is a view from a postcard sent to Selly Park on 31 August 1908.
　　　　　　　　　　　　　　　　　　　　　*Author's collection*

*Title Page:* A tram on a 39 service is ready to head into town when the inspector and conductor have had their discussion. Fresh bread and cakes are being unloaded in this scene which is dated 14th April 1938. The telegraph pole appears to have a protective white cover at the base.　Painting the base of posts white was later to be adopted during the war years to help pedestrians during the black-out.　　*H. B. Priestley*

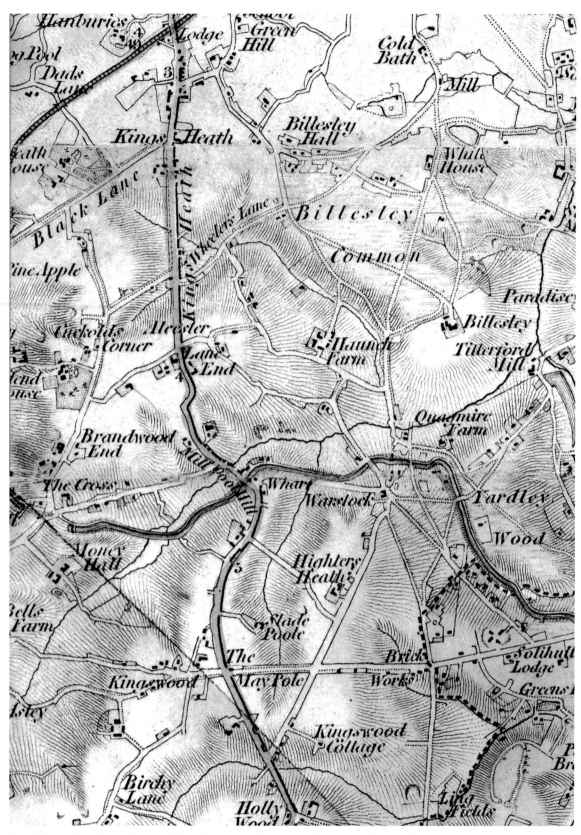

The King's Heath to Yardley Wood area as shown on this map dated c1860. Note Vicarage Road is then called Black Lane.

# INTRODUCTION

The idea of producing a second book was always a possibility as more material came my way soon after the first edition had gone onto the shelves. A number of people who bought the first book which is now out of print said it was the quality of the images that persuaded them to make the purchase. Thanks must go to the publisher and printer for the quality of the end product which I hope will make this edition just as attractive.

As with the first edition most of the images are from my extensive collection of old post cards purchased sometimes at great expense at post card fairs all around the country. I am also indebted to friends and readers of the first book for sending me their photographs from their early years in King's Heath.

Again we travel along the High Street and main areas of the village with a number of shop front images. We also journey from the Vicarage Road junction to the Maypole, around the side streets and onto the Yardley Wood area with more scenes at Happy Valley. There is also a new section on the Pineapple estate as I managed to secure a rare collection of early post cards from this area. This edition also includes images from the D. J. Norton collection and the Geoff Thompson Archive. These images are mainly from the 1950s and 1960s but this era is now around sixty years ago and is the period many people still remember with affection. There is the usual Sports and Leisure, Transport, Education and Public House sections as well as some more interesting railway material. I trust it will again be a good read and maybe provoke more readers comments.

# KING'S HEATH to THE MAYPOLE

Alcester Road (South) from the junction of Vicarage Road. Written on the reverse of this postcard was a wartime message from Herbert at Monyhull, 1st Southern General Hospital dated 25th January 1918. The strange post on the pavement to the left of the picture is a mystery but is thought to be a stench ventilation from the sewers below. The nearest three shops are Hedges chemist, Twigg's newsagents and Post Office and Arthur Jones glass merchant.

*Author's collection*


*Opposite:* A postcard view of 'Plas-Newydd', 50 Alcester Road (South). Sainsbury's and other retail shops were later built on this site. This postcard view was sent to Wednesbury on May 13th 1911.

*Author's collection*

A 1950s post card view of Alcester Road South with Kings the drapers prominent and a number 11 Outer Circle bus about to turn into Vicarage Road. *Author's collection*

An early postcard view of Alcester Road (South) from by Drayton Road. A three wheel vehicle, probably a Morgan is seen in the foreground but horse and carts still rule. *Author's collection*

Alcester Road south opposite Drayton
Road.  An Outer Circle No. 11 bus has just
come out of Addison Road. Arnold
Gender's Garage is just visible. Sainsbury's
and other modern businesses now dominate
this area.                        *courtesy Stan Budd*

Alcester Road looking towards the village near to Mossfield Road.                    *courtesy Stan Budd*

*Opposite top:* The cottages on Alcester Road near the junction with Howard Road. The cottages have long since disappeared and a children's play area now occupies the site.

*Author's collection*

*Opposite bottom:* Alcester Road looking towards the village from near Wheeler's Lane. It is almost deserted with the tram tracks dominating and two lads looking on.    *Author's collection*

ALCESTER RD. KINGS HEATH

ALCESTER LANES END.

Alcester Lanes End

Nº 1358

The Horse Shoe Inn appears to be doing good business on this summer's day. The area was always popular being by the canal and a short distance from 'Happy Valley'.                                        *courtesy Stan Budd*

*Opposite top:* A quiet scene at the tram terminus by the 'King's Arms' with just a bit of activity around the cart.                                        `                                        *Author's collection*

*Opposite bottom:* An early view of an almost deserted Alcester Lanes End. The card was sent to Canada on 6th July 1914 with the writer pointing out 'In picture notice block of buildings on left. The corner shop is now a large green grocer'.                                        *Author's collection*

Millpool Stores at 622 Alcester Road South on 8th February 1961. The newspaper bill boards fill the fence with the Birmingham Mail suggesting winnings of up to £700 on Place the Ball and the Radio Times advertising a new series of Churchill, the Valiant Years. Sadly, the shop and adjoining properties were swept away when the road was widened.                                                                                                                       *courtesy Geoff Thompson*

*Opposite top:* Maypole Garage c1940s. The garage was listed in the 1949 Kelly's directory as being at 1057 Alcester Road South close to the Maypole Pub.                                                              *courtesy Stan Budd*

*Opposite bottom:* The Maypole cross roads before any modern development. The view is looking towards Birmingham with Maypole Lane to the right.                                                              *courtesy Stan Budd*

# SUBURBIA AND SIDE STREETS

Dads Lane prior to any housing development on the right. Uffculme Park is to the left on this postcard sent to the Scilly Isles in 1928. *Author's collection*

*Opposite:* 45 Pineapple Road. This postcard view was sent to Headingley, Leeds in 1909. The brief Christmas wish ended saying 'This is a photo of our house'. More houses were later built in Pineapple Road and this house is now number 218. *Author's collection*

Shutlock Lane before any housing development.                                    *Author's collection*

Fordhouse Lane c1930. This postcard was part of the Pineapple Estate collection. It is titled King's Heath but would now be classed as Stirchley.                                    *Author's collection*

The old Billesley Arms. A view taken from a bedroom window along Brook Lane. *Author's collection*

The terraced houses near the bottom of Coldbath Road. The Outer Circle number 11 bus used to travel along here but due to the narrowness of the road the route was changed to run along Yardley Wood Road and Brook Lane. *Author's collection*

61 Coldbath Road. 11th May 1960. A little girl stands outside the Coldbath Stores situated midway down the road. The bay window of the terraced house to the left still has its original leaded lights.

*courtesy Geoff Thompson*

*Opposite top:* Brook Lane. Post card sent from 69, Vimy Road to Cheltenham, 9 August 1934. It is most likely the top part of Brook Lane looking towards Yardley Wood Road. The road is now widened along this stretch with a service road on the right. *Author's collection*

*Opposite bottom:* A postcard view of Swanshurst Lane c1940s. Swanshurst Park is to the right, and an outer circle No. 11 bus waits time at the bundy clock. *Author's collection*

BROOK LANE. BILLESLEY

SWANSHURST LANE.

Two early 1900s photographs of the Four Arches bridge on the River Cole by Brook Farm near to the bottom of the old Brook Lane. (See the early street map on page 23 for its location)

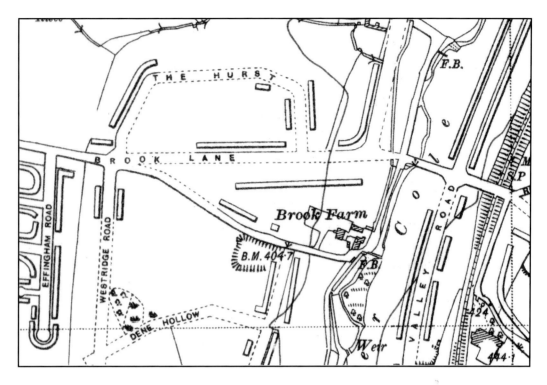

1930s map of Brook Farm area and Four Arches bridge marked F.B.

Woodthorpe Road looking towards Brandwood Road.                    *courtesy Stan Budd*

An early post card of May Lane published by H. B. Stainton, Alcester Lanes End Post Office. Early wooden fencing is prominent on both sides of the road. *Author's collection*

Taylor Road looking west from Haunch Lane. *Author's collection*

Monyhull Hall Road. This postcard was sent to a patient in Selly Oak Hospital on 6th November 1938.

*Author's collection*

Featherstone Road looking down to Alcester Road at the bottom with Hazelhurst and Livingstone road junction in the foreground. This early view is before the houses on the left were built. This postcard view was sent to Streatham, London on July 4th 1909.

*Author's collection*

Children stand for the photographer outside their house at 85 Livingstone Road in the early 1900s.  *courtesy Stephen Penker collection*

59 Brandwood Road in October 1965 prior to demolition in 1966.
*courtesy Stan Budd*

Old cottage in Grove Road near to the Red Lion.
*courtesy Stan Budd*

54 Addison Road. 29th April 1959. The garage, with proprietor W. J. Hackett was situated adjacent to residential properties. With today's health and safety regulations the proximity of the petrol pumps to the houses would certainly not now be allowed.
*courtesy Geoff Thompson*

GOLDSMITH ROAD KINGS HEATH

Goldsmith Road. My home where I grew up was number 5 on the left of this postcard view near to Institute Road and not a car in sight!

*Author's collection*

HEATHFIELD RD. KINGS HEATH.

Heathfield Road looking towards High Street.

*Author's collection*

The corner shop at 118 Springfield Road on 7th November 1960. This was before the age of the Supermarket when it was still a popular store and at the time under the ownership of K. Bloomfield.

*courtesy Geoff Thompson*

Poplar Road on 5th June 1961. The buildings above the shops appear rather grand with the exception of the green grocers shop on the left. Trade seems quiet at the launderette but the shoe repairer was always kept busy doing his leather soles and rubber heels.

*courtesy Geoff Thompson*

An early postcard view of Valentine Road looking down hill towards the start of High Street.

*Author's collection*

44 Ashfield Road January 1947. Outside the prefab are Harry Davis, with his wife Valda and first son Kenneth. There were nine prefabs built at this location at the junction of School Road and Ashfield Road. Prefabs in Birmingham were built between 1944 and 1948 to provide a quick solution to the lack of housing caused by the war. Over 4,600 were built but most had gone by the 1980s. Those in Wake Green Road remain however and are now Grade II listed.

*courtesy Brian Walsh & Mike Davis collection*

The off licence at 14 Silver Street on 15th May 1967. In the window there is an advertisement for draught gin at 33/11d a pint and whisky at 34/11d. Sadly, the shop and the cottage to the right no longer survive. Tommy Godwin's cycle shop is seen to the right.

*courtesy Geoff Thompson*

This undated view c1953 shows Waterloo Road close to its junction with York Road. Note how the petrol pumps are casually sited close to the front door of Waterloo Garage. All Saint's Church spire is just visible between the two blocks of houses.

*courtesy Geoff Thompson*

Vicarage Road 11ᵗʰ June 1954. These row of shops are at the Stirchley end of the Road near to the top of Kings Road. Hazelwell Garage features in this view.                                              *courtesy Geoff Thompson*

*Opposite top:*  This is G. M. Smallwood's shop on the corner of Silver Street and Fairfield Road on 7ᵗʰ March 1963.  This was one of the many small grocery shops which were found just a short walk from the main High Street shops.                                              *courtesy Geoff Thompson*

*Opposite bottom*:  This grocery shop at 40 Highbury Road on the corner of Silver Street was photographed on 5ᵗʰ January 1960, the proprietor being T. W. and E. F. Finch.

*courtesy Geoff Thompson*

# IN AND AROUND HIGH STREET

Bon Marche shop at 10 Poplar Road. A milliners shop with Harold Chambers proprietor c1914-17. The cyclist appears ready to deliver some new hats to customers. Note the carbide and oil lamps on his cycle. To the left at number 12 is John Hamilton Forsyth, Watchmaker.
*Author's collection*

*Opposite:* Walter Cookson stands proudly outside his shop at 15a Heathfield Road around 1918-20. It seems you could buy almost anything from his Newsagents shop, from postcards, hardware to fancy goods. Woodbine cigarettes and tobacco would also be a popular purchase.
*courtesy Patrick Hurley*

The interior of All Saint's church with inscribed arch. This post card view was sent to Burley in Wharfdale on 25th November 1911. *Author's collection*

An early 20th century photograph of the church choir at All Saint's. Some mothers and wives possibly make up the group. *courtesy Stan Budd*

A postcard view of High Street with the school and Institute on the right. This card was sent to the Isle of Wight May 31 1908.                                                                                  *Author's collection*

High Street during the 1950s with the road recently re-surfaced following the removal of the tram tracks. The school has now lost the top of the tower and F. W. Woolworth is doing good business in the old Institute building on the corner of Institute Road.                                                                       *Author's collection*

A postcard view of High Street from by the Hare & Hounds at the corner of York Road. This postcard view was sent to Northamptonshire on 12th June 1915. *Author's collection*

A typical High Street scene taken by Institute Road. This post card view was sent to Padstow in Cornwall on August 31st 1912. *Author's collection*

Just up from Poplar Road at 95 High Street was Mrs Lillie James, beer retailer. This view, taken c1920, shows Gladys Beames with child outside the front door.

*courtesy David Harris*

This 1970s view shows the row of shops in High Street prior to the re-development. Fosters shop is on the corner of Heathfield Road and a lone car sits at the curb on what looks like a quiet Sunday morning.

*Robin Jeynes*

The new W. H. Rhodes shop as designed by Craftinwood Ltd, Shopfitters in 1932.    *courtesy Terry Pearson*

*Opposite:*  This lovely shop front photograph of W. H. Rhodes is just up from the Hare & Hounds. Selling china, glass and pottery this view is probably dated around the 1920s and prior to its refurbishment. The sale notices have offers of 5/- to 10/- in the pound reductions. (25% to 50%).

*courtesy Terry Pearson*

This late 1960s, early 1970s view shows W. H. Rhodes shop still doing good business in the High Street. Parts of the original fancy pillars are still in evidence in this view. The three W. H. Rhodes shop photographs were supplied by the family of the late A. E. Pearson who was director of the company. *courtesy Terry Pearson*

*Opposite top:* Shopping in Tascos Branch 24 in the late 1940s. There is a choice of egg powder, fish paste and Mermaid oysters for this lady and sixty odd years ago Kellogg's cornflakes was already a regular buy. *Author's collection*

*Opposite bottom:* A group of children stand for the photographer opposite the Baptist chapel. The old cottages behind have now been replaced by a modern supermarket. *Author's collection*

Darlaston's Newsagent shop, 75 High Street on 17th August 1949. This paper Shop was there for quite a number of years as I remember as a child. The Kingsway Cinema is visible to the left where I spent every Saturday morning watching cowboy films and cartoons for the price of 6d (2½ p). You also had your name called out if it was your birthday. *courtesy Geoff Thompson*

*Opposite top:* High Street by the corner of Station Road on 6th November 1957. On the corner is Brown & Clark Ltd, Plumbers Merchants and in the offices above was Cecil Cariss, Auctioneers and Estate Agents. Next door is Kirk's, a sweet shop advertising home made ices and on the left is Brooks who claim to provide 'True London Tailoring'! *courtesy Geoff Thompson*

*Opposite bottom:* Redevelopment has started in this view opposite Institute Road on 27th October 1964. The long closed shops of Ault & Son and Chapman & Sanders are doomed but the buildings that contained W. E. Turner Ltd (footwear) and Marsh & Baxter survive to this day.

*courtesy Geoff Thompson*

*Above:* High Street in the early 1950s. A policeman on horseback passes another officer on his cycle whilst a bus on a 50B service passes swiftly by. The shops seem a little deserted and the tram tracks have yet to be removed. *courtesy Brian Walsh*

*Left:* Joan Thompson and Pat Bennett relax by the swing in Milford Place c1940s.

*courtesy Joan Walsh nee Thompson*

Joan Thompson and her friend Vicky Brown pose with their dolls pram in Milford Place in this view looking towards High Street in the 1940s.

*courtesy Joan Walsh nee Thompson*

A group of local children enjoy a party at All Saints to celebrate the coronation in 1953.

*courtesy Brian Walsh*

*Opposite top:* Removals were by horse and cart in October 1907 as this advertisement by F. Molesworth shows.

This popular King's Heath family butcher advertises in the local journal, April 1933.

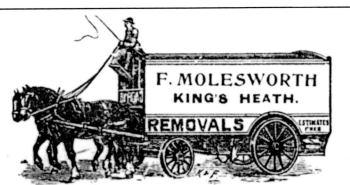

The demolition of the old Institute building has started in this view of October 1969. The swimming baths are still in business as a customer dashes up the steps to take the plunge. *Author's photograph*

ALLENS CROFT ROAD, PINE APPLE ESTATE.

THE SCHOOLS, PINE APPLE ESTATE.

# PINEAPPLE ESTATE

Pineapple Estate in 1925 as viewed from the railway line showing the junction of Allenscroft Road, Dawbwerry Road and Waldrons Moor. The three brickwork chimney stacks are still prominent in the distant around the Kings Road area. *courtesy Central Library, Local Studies and History Service*

Pineapple Estate was built in the 1920s. It was initially planned to be the first municipal housing estate in Birmingham when the land was bought in 1913 but the onset of the First World War postponed the start. The views in this chapter which are not credited are from a set of postcards bought by the author dating from around 1930.

*Opposite top:* Allenscroft Road.

*Opposite bottom:* Pineapple schools, now rebuilt and called Allenscroft school.

Bilberry Road.

St Mary Magdalen Church, Pineapple Estate. The United Church of England and Methodist Church at the Stirchley end of Vicarage Road was built in 1915.

Reeves Road. Children play happily on their scooters. St. Mary Magdalen church is visible on Vicarage Road.

The Green, at the junction with Vicarage Road.

Waldron Road.

Waldrons Moor. A distant view of the brick works chimney is seen in the Kings Road area.

Hazelwell pub in Pineapple Road as seen in 1961.

Vicarage Road shops on 21st December 1959. This row of shops is near to the junction of Allenscroft Road and has a fish shop, now called Pineapple chip Shop and two shops with prominent Cigarette advertising. At F. A. Harris, a television could be rented for just 7/6d a week but overall there doesn't appear to be a last minute pre Christmas shopping rush!

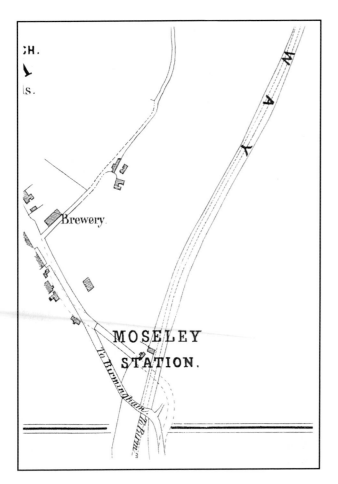

This is a section of a Midland Railway plan of 1861. It shows the original station, then called Moseley. When the railway was built, the road known as Welch's Hill was diverted over the newly erected Queen's Bridge. The turnpike road, previous to this diversion (the dotted line on the plan) took a circuitous course, and passed by the old house standing close to where the new station was built. In May 1933 an old resident of King's Heath informed the local paper of the fact that the Station Master's house was formerly the village inn known as the 'Fox & Dogs.'

This card was sent by the Station Master's wife Mrs Annie E Brayne on 29 April 1923. There were two cottages listed at the station in the 1901 census. George Wilkinson, a railway platelayer occupied the one cottage with his wife and four children. The other cottage was occupied by the Station Master, John Henry Brayne with his wife and three young children. *Author's collection*

WHAT A HEAD! BUT OH,
WHAT A NIGHT AT
KINGS HEATH.

# RAILWAY

A young railway porter awaits another arrival on the down platform c1906.          *Author's collection*

Child railway ticket dated
August 6th 1921.

An early Midland Railway ticket
from King's Heath to Brighton
Road dated October 1868.

Ballast Pit Sidings on 30th May 1955. These sidings were on the Moseley side of the Queen's Bridge. It is likely that this quarry was established when the line was built, the fact that stone was suitable for use as ballast being realised as the line was built through here – a useful find for the engineers. The sidings and quarry were certainly in use by 1854, when the Inspector of PW was reported for obstructing the main line with ballast trains.

*D. J. Norton*

The weighbridge in the station yard is undergoing heavy maintenance. The health and safety rope has not deterred the young children! c. July 1964.

*T. Ross/Kidderminster Railway Museum*

Leslie Williams poses in the doorway of the Frederick Sharp coal office in the early 1920s. The office was previously under the ownership of Dixon & Baker.

*courtesy Michael Williams*

A mid-1960s view of the station drive with a varied selection of coal merchants offices. The house coal trade was still important at this time.

*courtesy Doug Taylor*

*Opposite top:*  Class 4F No. 44087 of Gloucester shed is seen passing through King's Heath on 18th September 1955 hauling a load of empty mineral wagons probably bound for Washwood Heath.

*D. J. Norton*

*Opposite bottom:*  44598 of Nottingham shed powers through King's Heath with a freight on 27th January 1952. These down trains were often banked up the gradient to King's Heath.  43812 of Saltley shed, a bank pilot engine from a previous train is seen in the small siding awaiting a path back down to Washwood Heath.

*D. J. Norton*

*Below:*  The weigh bridge office with a Winchester coal lorry behind in June 1966.  Winchester coal merchants were operating from the yard for approximately 26 years from 1948 until 1973.

*Roger Carpenter collection*

Class 8F No. 48635 from Nottingham shed heads west through King's Heath with a mineral train. Another Loco crew stand by the signal box probably waiting for a path back down to Washwood Heath with their banking engine.

*D. J. Norton*

44814 heads a passenger train south through Hazelwell
Station on 5th May 1953.                    *D. J. Norton*

*Opposite bottom:* The signalman's Reliant stands at the rear
of the signal box on a sunny day in 1966.

                                        *M. A. King*


Signalman Len works the levers in Hazelwell signal box
on 22nd March 1964.              *Author's collection*

# William Blower (Late ⎯⎯⎯ Thomas Hookham)

**Coal Merchant,**

Celebrated Cannock Chase, etc. Other Coals; Coke, Slack, Breeze, etc. ⎯⎯⎯

Orders by post or left at office receive prompt attention. ⎯⎯⎯

Price lists on application. Truck loads to any Station.

## KING'S HEATH STATION WHARF.

Coal Merchant William Blower advertises in the local Journal, December 1907.

# CHEAP  TRIPS

### From MOSELEY AND KING'S HEATH.

### WHITSUNTIDE HOLIDAYS.

| | Departure Times | |
|---|---|---|
| | From Moseley | From King's Heath |
| **WHIT SUNDAY, MAY 20th.** | a.m. | a.m. |
| Bristol (5/6), Weston-Super-Mare (6/-) .. .. | 11.15 | 11.20 |
| | | a.m. |
| Alton (for Alton Towers) (3/6) .. .. .. | N.B. | 10.5 |
| **MONDAY, MAY 21st.** | | |
| Rhyl (9/-), Colwyn Bay /9/6), Llandudno (10.-) .. | 6.8 | 6.4 |
| Bath (8/-), Bournemouth (12/-) .. .. .. .. | N.B. | 6.35 |
| Cheltenham (4/6), Gloucester (5/6), Bristol (8/-), | | |
| Weston-Super-Mare (9/-) .. .. | N.B. | 7.45 |
| | a.m. p.m. | a.m. p.m. |
| Salford Priors (2/6), Harvington (2/6*), Evesham (3/-) | 9.15 12.36 | 9.19 12.40 |
| (* 3/- from Moseley.) | | |
| Worcester (2/6) .. .. .. .. | 9.35 12.49 | 9.40 12.52 |
| | a.m. | a.m. |
| Ashchurch (4/-), Tewkesbury (4/-) .. .. | 9.53 | 9.40 |
| Malvern Link (3/-*), Great Malvern (3/-*) .. .. | 9.53 | 9.57 |
| (* 3/6 from Moseley.) . | | |
| | a.m. p.m. | a.m. p.m. |
| Sutton Park (1/4) .. .. .. .. | 9.58 12.23 | 9.54 12.19 |
| **WHIST MONDAY AND TUESDAY, MAY 21st and 22nd.** | | |
| Barnt Green (for the Lickeys) (1/-), 6d. after 5.0 p.m. | Various. | Various. |
| **WHIT TUESDAY, MAY 22nd.** | | |
| | | a.m. |
| Alton (for Alton Towers) (3/6) .. .. .. | N.B. | 11.25 |
| | a.m. p.m. | a.m. p.m. |
| Salford Priors (2/6), Harvington (2,6*), Evesham (3.-) | 11.33 12.49 | 11.35 12.52 |
| (* 3/- from Moseley.) | | |

N.B.—Where no departure times are shown there are no bookings.
See handbills for particulars of cheap trips to Redditch, Alcester, Broom Junction, Defford, Eckington, Bredon, etc., etc.

Full particulars from L.M.S. Stations and Agencies.

ALL LOCAL CHEAP FACILITIES WILL BE IN FORCE THROUGHOUT THE HOLIDAYS.

**Penny-a-Mile " Summer " Tickets Available.**
**Anywhere.   Any Day.   Any Train.**

L. M. S. Cheap Trips advertisement in the local Journal, May 18th 1938.

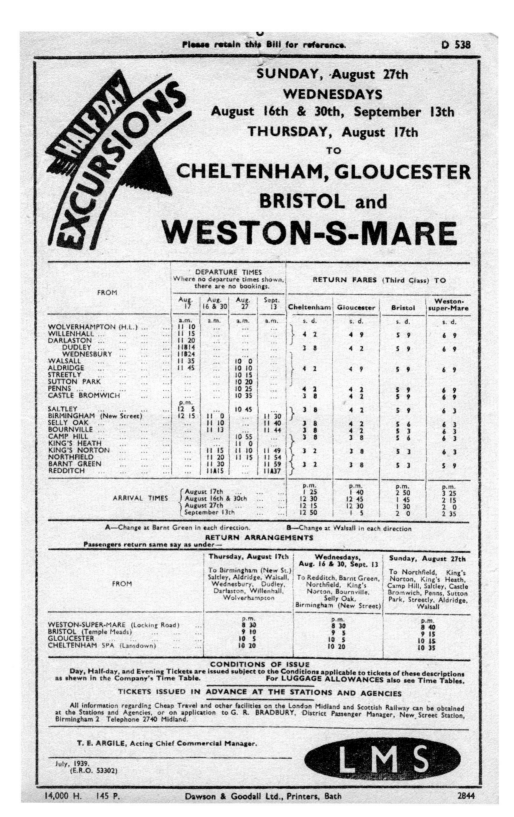

An LMS Half Day excursion leaflet from King's Heath and other local stations to Weston-Super-Mare. The leaflet is dated July 1939, just two months before the outbreak of World War ll. The train was booked to leave King's Heath at 11 o clock and the fare to Weston was six shillings and 3 pence. (31p).

# TRANSPORT

The driver and conductor wait time at the Maypole terminus on 29th August 1949 before heading off to Station Street with the 35 service.                                                   *T. J. Edgington*

*Opposite:*  A tram on the 42 route heads towards town on 9th July 1949. The open balcony used to be my favourite place to travel whatever the weather. This tram No. 409 carries an advert for G. R. Bailey, the popular bakers and confectioners of High Street King's Heath.        *T. J. Edgington*

A bus on a 50 service passes the Vicarage Road junction in the 1950s. There is not much traffic around and the traffic lights had yet to be installed. *Alan B. Cross*

Bus HOV 666 on 13A service is seen in School Road Yardley Wood close to the terminus about 1961-2. For those who know their buses this is is a Leyland Titan PD2/1 with a Brush H30/24R body dating from the end of 1947. *R.H.G. Simpson*

This bus in Vicarage Road is on the Outer circle route but only going as far as Coventry Road.

*Robert F. Mack*

Three buses head down the High Street close to the junction with Bank Street c1950s.

*Robert F. Mack*

*Opposite top:* The bus terminus in Haunch Lane on 22nd May 1955. The bus on the 18A route waits while a small queue stand at the bus stop on the Yardley Wood Road for their journey towards town. The 18A bus lay-by has now gone as well as the vintage bus shelter and the telephone kiosks on the Yardley Wood Road.                                                                                                                    *D. J. Norton*

*Opposite bottom:* Fitters, cleaners and tram crew pose in front of steam engine No. 56 in Silver Street, 1892.                                                                                                                                                                   *Clarence Gilbert collection*

A steam tram engine and carriage is ready to set off from Silver Street in 1888.          *Clarence Gilbert collection*

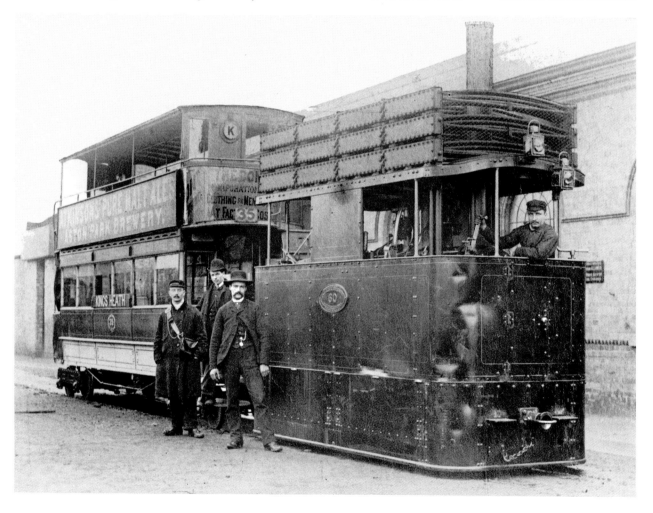

Steam tram No. 41 stands in the Silver Street depot in 1888. The foreman with his large spanner may have just made some adjustments.
*Clarence Gilbert collection*

*Opposite top:* A mucky street scene! But this is how they used to be. A steam tram is about to start its journey into town in 1905 when the business of taking the photograph is completed. King's Heath school is seen behind the tram. This was to be the last year of steam tram operation as 1906 saw the conversion to electric traction.
*Clarence Gilbert collection*

*Opposite bottom:* A group of workers stand for the photographer in this 1889 scene at the Silver Street depot.
*Clarence Gilbert collection*

A steam tram waits by the junction of Reddings Road before dropping down Welch's Hill to King's Heath and the terminus at Silver Street in 1906, before the introduction of electric traction. The trams advertises the Bordesley Palace Theatre with twice nightly performances. *Clarence Gilbert collection*

Ten years earlier a report in the Moseley and King's Heath Journal reported the following:

"At last the Birmingham Central Tramways Company have found a way out of the difficulty Welch's Hill way! No longer will be witnessed the scene of a man waving a flag by day and a lamp by night, in order to let the King's Heath tram drivers know that the course is clear. No one, I should think, could have been more ashamed of this antiquated system—quite out of character in this nineteenth century—than Mr. Holmden, the general manager of the company. Unless possessing a heart of stone, no one could help having pity on the cripple, who on a cold winter's day looked an object of pity. His lot, on such occasions, was even more trying than that experienced by Nansen and his companions at the North Pole. Possibly Mr. Holmden in reading an account of these arctic explorers was reminded of the poor signalman's lot, and so "hurried up" the matter, quite apart from the police court proceedings! The way out of the difficulty has been found by the Central Tramways Co. purchasing a small plot of land belonging to the Midland Railway Co., and adjoining the last of the villas on Welch's Hill. On this piece of land a signal box has been erected and inside this the man works a semaphore. It is to be hoped that the signalman will not take undue advantage of his exalted position by indulging in an afternoon nap!"

Three trams wait just short of Alcester Lanes End on 1st October 1949 for the returning crowds from King's Heath Dog Track meeting. For the drivers and conductors it is time for a chat and to pose for the photographer.

*A. N. H. Glover, courtesy Alan Wycherley*

A tram on the 42 service to Alcester Lanes End speeds into King's Heath High Street by the junction of Queensbridge Road on 19th April 1947. *T. J. Edgington*

# SPORT & LEISURE

Alcester Lanes End looking towards Maypole showing the entrance to King's Heath Dog Track on the left. A police officer on horseback is approaching on this otherwise deserted scene in the 1960s.

*courtesy Andrew Maxam*

*Opposite:* Young children pose in costume for the camera of Albert Edward Dawson.

*Author's collection*

King's Heath Park Lodge. Post card sent to St Helier on 29th April 1926. The sender complained of rough sea crossing on recent visit to Jersey. *Author's collection*

The photographer has attracted quite some interest across the pond in King's Heath Park on this postcard sent to Swansea in 1925. *Author's collection*

A fancy dress event outside Happy Valley tea rooms. This post card view is by J. J. Crook of 85 Taylor Road King's Heath.

*Author's collection*

Children dress up for the Yardley Wood May Festival in 1932.

*Author's collection*

This prize winning Tradesman's Turnout shows Charles Henry Adkins on his pony and trap at the King's Heath horse show around 1921. Mr. Adkins had a number of Butchers shops in Moseley area and was also chairman of the King's Heath Horse Show Society.

*courtesy The King's Heath Horse Show Society*

Another smiling winner at the King's Heath Horse Show on 25th May 1953.

*Author's collection*

KINGS HEATH HORSE SHOW SOCIETY
OFFICERS AND COUNCIL 1921.

T.A.CHECKLEY  A.W.GORE  J.S.SEELEY  J.HOLLIS  W.WALFORD  E.E.DIGWOOD  J.BERTRAM  G.PRATT  W.A.MARSH  W.E.WELLINGS
W.F.BARR  J.MARKHAM  A.W.LASHFORD  A.G.SAKER  F.A.BULLOCK  H.WEBB  A.HOXTON  A.E.BULLOCK  F.G.HOWIS  A.R.PERRETT  F.WEBSTER  WOOD.
COL.W.E.LAWRENCE  COL.FOSTER  C.H.ADKINS  MAJOR J.HOWARD CARTLAND, J.P.  G.H.BULLOCK  A.A.JORDISON  F.LLOYD.

This photograph by A. E. Dawson of Station Road King's Heath shows the full Officers and Council of the King's Heath Horse Show Society in 1921. Some well known local dignitaries are present in the group.

*courtesy Vernon Fisher*

King's Heath Early Morning School cricket team pose with their shield after winning the league in 1910.

*Author's collection*

The tennis courts at the recreation grounds, Alcester Lanes End. The houses in May Lane are seen in the background.                                                                    *Author's collection*

An early view of the Carnegie Library, High Street.                    *Author's collection*

The Divisional Boys Brigade Parade marches along the High Street in 1956 with officer Mr S Bagshaw, Sergeants Roger Gough and Roy Savery at the head.

*courtesy 6<sup>th</sup> Coy BB*

The 6<sup>th</sup> Boys Brigade camp in the 1950s.  There is some doubt as to the actual year.  Records say Rhossilli in 1952, but I would say it is Tenby 1953 with the fair-haired author in the centre behind the officers.

*courtesy 6<sup>th</sup> Coy BB*

This press photograph shows a large crowd enjoying the dog racing at King's Heath in 1926. The report went on to say. 'The new sport of greyhound racing after mechanical hares driven round the track in front of them by an electric motor has gained amazing popularity in this country, and courses are being opened in all parts. The picture shows a competing dog taking a jump in fine style during a race at the opening of the new course at King's Heath, Birmingham'.

*Author's collection*

*Opposite top:* King's Heath House is the scene for this group of Sunday School teachers in 1908.

*courtesy Stan Budd*

*Opposite bottom:* This A. E. Dawson photograph shows a wedding group in the King's Heath area taken possibly in the Edwardian era of the early 1900s. Can anyone recognise their ancestors?

*Author's collection*

Dorothy Cartland on her cycle with younger sister Geraldine at Hazelwell Hall around 1903.
*courtesy Stan Budd*

Three young lads pose for the camera near the entrance to King's Heath Park at the corner of Vicarage Road and Avenue Road. The lad in the centre appears to be holding the cameraman's tripod. This post card was sent to Dollar in Scotland on 6th May 1916 from Tudor House, All Saint's Road. *Author's collection*

It's party time in Fairfield Road during the Coronation celebrations of 1953. Residents are enjoying the atmosphere of a fancy dress event. The huge tent was obviously an insurance in case of inclement weather and stretched right across the road.

*courtesy Bob Chedgzoy*

Fairfield Road residents celebrating VE Day at the end of the Second World War. The group are standing in front of the pool in King's Heath Park. The photograph was supplied by Bob Chedgzoy (fifth from left, front row) who can name practically everyone else in the picture. Are you one of the other young children?

*courtesy Bob Chedgzoy*

A group of Westfield Road residents are enjoying their sit in a Jeep during 1949.

*courtesy Joan Walsh nee Thompson*

The Parade and Kingsway picture house near the town end of the High Street. This fairly modern post card view was sent to Leamington Spa in September 1956. There are a few cars about but compared to today the scene is quite deserted.

*Author's collection*

## THE KINGSWAY CINEMA
HIGH STREET.                    Telephone : SOUth 1352

Whit. Monday, June 10th—3 Days.

SYDNEY HOWARD AND NANCY CARROLL
in
**" Transatlantic Merry Go Round "** (A)

Thursday, Friday, and Saturday.
LAUREL AND HARDY
in
**" Babes in Toyland "** (U)

Whit. Monday : MATINEE 2.45 p.m.
Evening :        FIRST HOUSE 6 p.m.        } Not
                 SECOND HOUSE 8.30 p.m. } Continuous.

The Kingsway Cinema advertises its programme on 7th June 1935.

An advertisement for the Ideal Picture House in the High Street from a local Journal of May 1914.

## 'IDEAL' Picture House
HIGH STREET. KINGS HEATH.
**The Premier Picture House of Kings Heath.**
Manager    -    ERNEST ELLERSLIE.

**THE WORLD'S BEST PICTURES**

Perfectly Projected on a Silver Screen.

Popular Prices - 3d. and 6d.

**CONTINUOUS PERFORMANCE**
Every Evening 6-30 to 10-30 (Sats. 6)
MATINEES—
MONDAYS & WEDNESDAYS, 3
Special CHILDREN'S PERFORMANCE
Saturdays, 2-30. Admission 1d. & 2d.

DRAMA, COMEDY, TRAVEL, EDUCATIONAL and TOPICAL FILMS.

A Wheelers Lane Boys School photograph of the author c1952 sporting his 'Ian Allan Locospotters' badge. In 1953 he left school to start work at Cadbury Bros. at Bournville.

# EDUCATION

Colmore Road Primary School. Another A E Dawson photograph, this time of Group seven pupils in the playground. The background is still rural with fields and trees where houses had yet to be built.

*Author's collection*

*Opposite bottom:* This is Colmore Road Council School during the First World War. At this time it was in use as a Temporary Military Hospital, pupils being taught at King's Heath School Institute Road. This postcard view of October 1918 was sent to Carlisle by a patient who wrote 'Dear Sarah. Just a line to let you know I am still keeping well. This is the hospital where we are. My wound is mending alright but I am still in bed.'

*Author's collection*

King's Heath Junior School, Institute Road seen from the top of the partly demolished Institute c1969.

*courtesy Stan Budd*

*Opposite top:* Wheelers Lane Junior football team 1946-7. Mr. Flavell Head teacher is on the right at the back and Mr Baines, back left was the coach. Some names mentioned by Patrick Hurley, who is front left, are: - Gordon 'Nipper' Hunt, front right, and Clive Bloxham, second left, back row. Clive ran a vegetable shop with his father in Heathfield Road and the tall fair-haired lad seated front right was, I think, one of the Winchester lads, possibly John. *courtesy Patrick Hurley*

*Opposite bottom:* The Wheeler's Lane Junior football team, 1966-7 season. *courtesy Peter Topley*

King's Heath Junior & Infant school Institute Road seen from the air. *courtesy Stan Budd*

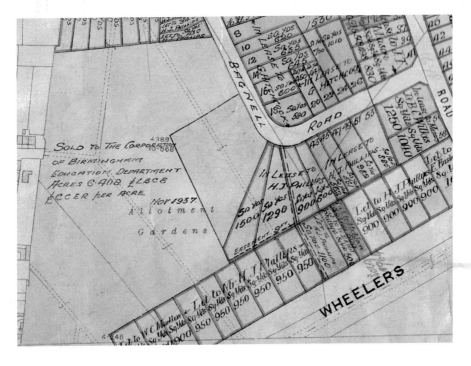

A surveyors plan of the Bagnell Road, Wheelers Lane area of 1937 showing the allotment gardens site which was sold to the Corporation of Birmingham Education Department for the building of the Wheelers Lane schools. The acreage was 6.408 but the cost per acre appears to be in code. The total area of each new house is shown in square yards.

Brandwood Lodge School advertisement for 11th January 1935.

# BRANDWOOD LODGE SCHOOL
## Brandwood Road,
## KING'S HEATH.

Spring Term: Thursday, January 17th.

**BOYS and GIRLS 4—12 Years.**

Sound Modern Education and Preparation for Public Schools. Successes at Entrance Examinations 1930-1931-1932-1933-1934.

Principal—Miss ELSIE COOPER, L.L.A.

**18A** 'Bus passes the School· Pupils escorted to and from 'Buses and Trams if desired.

This class of junior children at Institute Road School c1940s appear to be working on their model theatres. Some class mates remembered by Joan Walsh (back right) are John Barlow, Linda Brown, Bethany Vincent and Pamela Panter.

*courtesy Joan Walsh nee Thompson*

The Billesley Arms

# PUBLIC HOUSES

The Billesley Hotel c1950s, which at this time was still known locally as The Billesley Arms.

*Author's collection*

*Opposite top:* The King's Arms, Alcester Lanes End. This early scene is depicted on a postcard sent to Carnarvon in September 1909. The licensee at this time was Thomas Henry Graves. The tram, in the early years of electric traction is waiting to depart on its journey to Hill Street. *Author's collection*

*Opposite bottom:* The old Billesley Arms. *Author's collection*

The early Hare & Hounds pub c1880. Standing outside is the tenant landlord, Levi Cottrell and looking out from the upstairs window is his wife, Susan.
*courtesy Kathleen Cottrell*

The lawn in the garden at the rear of the Hare & Hounds c1880s where once the game of quoits was played.
*courtesy Kathleen Cottrell*

A group pose in the gardens at the rear of the Hare & Hounds. The landlord, Levi Cottrell is seen leaning on the bench fourth from left. Seen behind are a row of arbours where customers could enjoy their drinks in the summer.
*courtesy Kathleen Cottrell*

An early view of the rebuilt Hare & Hounds with the barrow boy prominent in York Road.

*courtesy Carl Chinn, Birmingham Lives Archive*

The new 'Cross Guns Hotel'. A postcard view sent from the 'Cross Guns' on 17th February 1910. The message reads 'Please find enclosed postal order for 2/- for hamper of fish as advertised to above address'.

*Author's collection*

The new Warstock pub on the corner of Prince of Wales Lane and Yardley Wood Road.

*Author's collection*

Two interior views of the Maypole public house showing the Gents Smoke Room (*top*) and the Assembly Room (*bottom*).                    *courtesy Stan Budd*

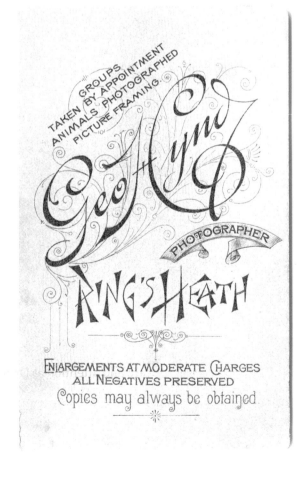

# EARNING A LIVING

The workforce of John Gibbs Ltd at 25 Grange Road c1920s.  An Albert Edward Dawson photograph.

*Author's collection*

*Opposite top:*  Receiving care and attention at Druids Farm Maypole.          *Author's collection*

*Opposite bottom:*  George Hynd was another prolific photographer in King's Heath. Here we see one of his portraits of a woman holding a Cyclist's Touring Club handbook, and next to it, the reverse side of the Carte de visite photograph.  *Author's collection*

# The Lukeman's Forge

Charles Lukeman, trained as a blacksmith at the forge of J. Hall, Stirchley Street at the site of present 'Three Horse Shoes' Pub. He later went on to set up his own forge at the town end of the Parade, 47 High Street, King's Heath (see photograph in first edition). His sign read – 'C. Lukeman, Late foreman to A.L. Gibson Vet' surgeon, Birmingham. Horses carefully shod and jobbing work attended to'.

The business eventually transferred to another site in King's Heath. A letter from about 1903-4 giving notice of removal and still in the family's possession reads:

> 'King's Heath. Dear Sir or Madam, We beg to inform you that we have moved our shoeing and general smithing and wheelwright business from High Street to the new and more convenient premises at No.1 Yard, Grange Road, near High Street. All orders will be promptly attended to. We take this opportunity of thanking you for your patronage in the past and hoping to receive a continuance of your favours in the future. We are, yours respectfully, C. Lukeman & Sons'.

In 1905 Grange Road and High Street were still in use, but in 1906 the High Street site had closed.

On 17th March 1907, aged 52, Charles Lukeman passed away. The eldest son Joe set up his own forge at Rednal. Emily (Grandmother) carried on the forge in Grange Road, which was in her name until 1910. From 1913 to 1915 Emily was in partnership with her son Alec at 19a York Road.

In about 1924 Alec Lukeman moved into larger premises at 31a York Road, which was 60ft long and 40ft wide. The forge made wheels, wagons, fencing, and iron tables.

In 1938 Alec retired and gave the business and tools to Mr. George Batchelor, who had worked for him for many years. Unfortunately, Mr. Batchelor and his family were killed in an air raid in King's Heath in 1940, when a bomb fell on their house in Alfred Street (see photograph opposite). Alec Lukeman died in 1955.

This was the later forge in either Grange or York Road c1907 – 1915. *Author's collection*

The Batchelor and Panker families happily face the camera in Alfred Street. Albert Road houses are seen behind. The Batchelor family with the exception of one child were unfortunately killed when their house in Alfred Street was bombed in an air raid c1940.

*courtesy Lukeman family*

Charles & Emily Lukeman (Blacksmiths) c1900.
*courtesy Lukeman family*

## Pure Milk !
## Fresh Milk !

JAMES HENRY WOODWARD,

OF

## "COLD=BATH" FARM

### STONEY LANE, MOSELEY,

DELIVERS THE ABOVE **TWICE** DAILY IN MOSELEY AND
KINGS HEATH, DIRECT FROM MILCH COWS ON
THE FARM.

Summer Price, **3d.** per Quart.

Winter    „    **3½d.**    „

——— SPECIAL **EARLY** DELIVERIES TO ALL PARTS. ———

### HIGH=CLASS DAIRY PRODUCE:

## Cream, Butter, New-laid Eggs,

ETC., ETC.

NOTE THE ADDRESS:

### The only "Cold=Bath" Farm,

STONEY LANE, MOSELEY

NATIONAL TELEPHONE 147 Y.

Cold-Bath Farm advertise their quality milk in April 1903. Stoney Lane later became Yardley Wood Road at this point.

*Opposite top:* The King's Heath Model Dairy staff pose for the camera of Albert Edward Dawson c1920.
*Author's collection*

*Opposite bottom:* Bailey's Confectioners workshop situated at the rear of their shop at 151 High Street
*courtesy Stan Budd*

# YARDLEY WOOD AND HAPPY VALLEY

Bampton Pool which was also known as Priory Mill Pool. This view is looking South with Priory Mill behind the photographer.

*Author's collection*

*Opposite top:* A wedding group photograph of Stanley Overton's Aunt outside 86 Prince of Wales Lane.

*courtesy Stanley Overton*

*Opposite bottom:* A young Alan Overton on the bonnet of his uncle Wally Smith's Wolseley in the area behind the Warstock Pub which is seen behind. Wally was a bus driver at Yardley Wood bus garage. This area behind the houses had a number of garages and little workshops. c1949.

*courtesy Stanley Overton*

PRIORY MILL, YARDLEY WOOD.

A peaceful scene showing Priory Mill Yardley Wood.

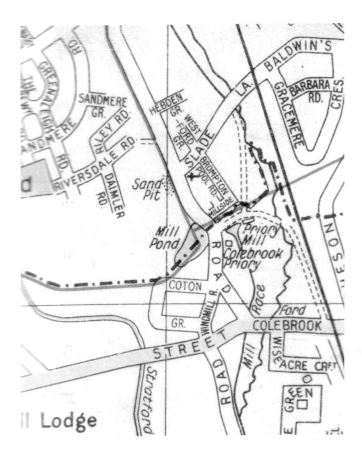

An early street map showing Priory Mill and pool.

Looking west along the canal at Yardley Wood. This is a view on a postcard sent to Canada in August 1906, the writer mentions Alice Bunn and Ettie watching poor Bob in the water.

*Author's collection*

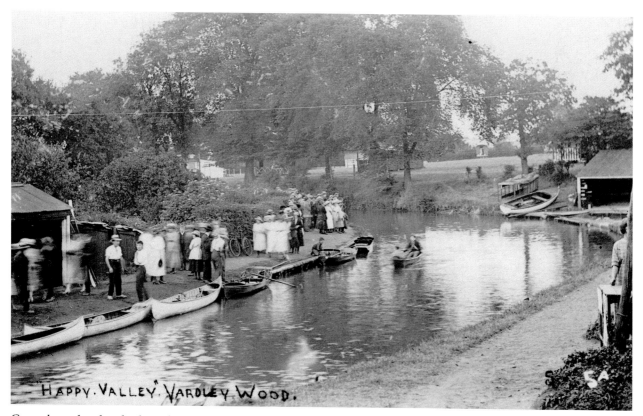

"HAPPY. VALLEY" YARDLEY WOOD.

Crowds gather by the boat house at Happy Valley.

*Author's collection*

A view of Happy Valley looking west towards the old Yardley Wood Road bridge. This postcard was sent on August 5 1913.

*Author's collection*

## Happy Valley bridge at Yardley Wood

The old road bridge over the canal at Happy Valley was demolished on 25th September 1936. The Birmingham Gazette of 26th September 1936 reported the event of 'The Bridge That Would Not Give In'. The report went on to say:

This bridge all but beat the engineers who signed its destruction........For years notices have stood on each side of the bridge, a narrow arched, hump-backed structure at Happy Valley, Yardley Wood, proclaiming (under the Motor-car Acts, 1896 and 1903) that the bridge is "insufficient" to carry a vehicle of more than five tons weight or a vehicle and trailer of more than eight tons combined.

Yesterday, engineers piled on tons and tons and then waited hours before cracks appeared-and then, when the weight on the bridge had reached 126 ½ tons, a portion-only a portion-of the arch fell in.

The bridge which is over the Stratford Canal is not beautiful, but, my goodness! It was strong! Incidentally, it was built 147 years ago (In 1789).

The engineers on the demolition task--officials of the Department of Scientific and Industrial Research--had tortured the bridge for over a week past, exerting pressure of 20 tons on it periodically to see just how it would react, in the hope that the information thus gained would help them to decide the fate of other similar bridges throughout the country. Up to yesterday the most that the bridge yielded then was 3/100 inch!

Then they set out to demolish it, with the idea of seeing just how much it would stand.....and the gallant bridge did not give up without a struggle, without doing its best to obtain a reprieve for its comrades under sentence

The engineers had rigged up apparatus with which to "kill" the bridge. Huge girders rested on massive baulks of timber placed on each side of the bridge and on top rested 120 tons of pig-lead.

### PAIN IN THE NECK!

Between the girders and the concrete strips on the floor of the bridge were large hydraulic jacks, and it was when these jacks were set working that ,unable to push up against the weight of girders and lead-135 tons in all-they pushed down and gave the bridge an awful pain in the neck!

And this was how the gallant bridge fought for its life:

The engineers started "loading" at 12.10p.m.

**Ten tons—the bridge didn't mind in the slightest;**
**Twenty tons—still going strong;**
**Thirty tons—one wee crack over the arch in the centre;**
**Forty tons—the crack grew a little longer;**
**Fifty tons—the crack was lengthening;**
**Sixty tons—the pump working the hydraulic jacks broke down and the bridge won—temporarily!**

## MORE AND MORE

The battle was resumed when the pump was repaired. The engineers added to the bridges burden:

**Seventy tons—the bridge squeaked a protest that this wasn't quite playing the game;**

**Eighty tons—the engineers expected a fall, but the bridge just didn't oblige.**

**Eighty-eight and a half tons—the bridge won again when one of the hydraulic jacks weaker than the bridge gave up the ghost and snapped in halves.**

I thought that the bridge should have the verdict; that the death sentence should be commuted; but the engineers were of another frame of mind.

When a bridge at Derby—and that a bridge built of masonry with approved key-stone design, as opposed to the brick bridge of Yardley Wood succumbed to only 80 tons—well, this humble bridge couldn't be allowed to better them.

## THE LAST STRAW

So they fitted up another jack and put the screw on again.

90 tons.....100 tons....110......125 "The bridge is going to win!" exclaimed Yardley Wood folk gathered around watching the battle.

But then came the last straw; another one-and-a-half tons was applied—the absolute maximum if the jacks were not to lift the load of girders and lead and, the engineers feared, tip them over into the canal, instead of exerting their pressure upon the bridge.

**126 ½ tons....and then bits of plaster and mortar began to fall from inside the arch. The bridge wasn't dead yet, however, and that load had to be maintained for over an hour before....."Cameras!" cried Dr. Davey, of the National Physical Research Laboratories, who was in charge of the work, and a score of cameras—press, newsreels, cinema and just plain snap-shot—clicked to catch the picture of the underpart of one side of the bridge falling away.**

## AFTER SIX HOURS

The brickwork crashed on to the timber platform erected under the bridge across two barges; fibrous roots of a tree 15 yards away hung from the gap...the engineers were satisfied, at 6.5pm, called it a day after a six hour battle with a bridge that gave as good as it received.

Contractors will now step in and dismantle the bridge, and soon Yardley Wood will have a fine level 65- foot wide structure. But many will remember and mourn The Bridge That Wouldn't Give In.

A 26th September 1936 Birmingham Gazette press photograph of the Happy Valley bridge showing the maximum weight limit warning of 8 tons.

The gardens at Happy Valley with the Arcade to the right. This postcard was sent to Huddersfield in 1924. The message reads. 'You would enjoy yourself here, we are close to a Common and a few minutes walk from this place and surrounded by fields'. *Author's collection*

An open air dance at Happy Valley. *Author's collection*

The Refreshment Rooms by the canal at Happy Valley. This building was also known as the 'People's Empire Club' and boxing was also held there. The big white gate led to Yardley Wood Road or Stoney Lane as it was earlier known. This postcard view was sent to Perry Barr in August 1913. *Author's collection*

The Queen Victoria Jubilee seat at the junction of School Road and Warstock Lane. Warstock Lane is off to the right and Highters Heath Lane to the left.

*Author's collection*

Jubilee Seat, Yardley Wood.

Three young men named on the postcard as Walter White, Tom Chapman and Donald.....enjoy their holiday break at Happy Valley just prior to the First World War. *Author's collection*

The King Edward pleasure boat awaits customers on the canal at Happy Valley. *Author's collection*

The River Cole ford on the Yardley Wood Road. A crowd gather on the footbridge to watch the photographer.

*Author's collection*

Young rowers relax after taking some boating exercise on the canal at Happy Valley.  *Author's collection*

Peterbrook Road Yardley Wood with a very ornate castellated residence on the right and a small corn mill on the left earlier described as an Oatmeal Mill. It was probably only used for grinding grain and this was mainly for animal feed. "The Castle" as it was known by the local people was in fact the stables for the miller's house which was close by. The stables were built by Stanbury Eardley at the turn of the nineteenth and twentieth centuries. The ground floor was the coach house and stables with the accommodation for groom above. Stanbury Eardley was a lawyer from Birmingham and by all accounts was a bit of a character. He was a tall man who dressed in the manner of Charles I and rode a black horse to the office in Birmingham. He was passionate about the horse so he bought the field next to the miller's house on which he built the magnificent stables, coach house and groom quarters. It is rumoured that when his horse died, it was buried in the field standing upright. To fund all this work, it eventually became apparent that he had been embezzling funds from his clients and he was arrested, tried and sent to gaol. Modern houses are now prominent in this area which now comes under the district of Solihull Lodge. This postcard view, produced by Chapman & Sanders, High Street, King's Heath, was sent from 85 Goldsmith Road to Matlock Bath, Derbyshire on October 23rd 1908. The sender writes, 'This is a view of your Uncle's old mill.'                              *Author's collection*

*Opposite top:* An old postcard view of the Drawbridge on the Yardley Wood canal near to the Aqueduct.
*Author's collection*

*Opposite bottom:* Young girls enjoy a relaxing time at 'Aqueduct Walk', Yardley Wood.
*Author's collection*

DRAWBRIDGE, SHIRLEY
- ON YARDLEY WOOD CANAL -

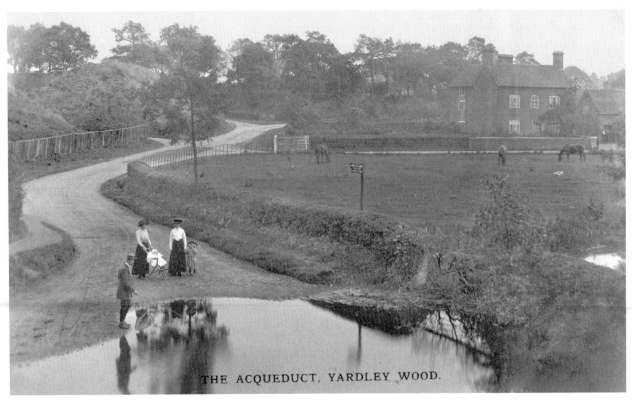

THE ACQUEDUCT, YARDLEY WOOD.

An old postcard view of the area looking south-east by the Aqueduct near Yardley Wood.

*Author's collection*

An unknown location possibly on the River Cole in the Yardley Wood area. This postcard view was sent from King's Heath to an officer of the Royal North West Mounted Police in Calgary, Canada on May 23 1906.

*Author's collection*

An early postcard view showing Priory Road looking south. *Author's collection*

A peaceful scene by the cottages in Slade Lane, looking towards the River Cole crossing.   This is a view from a postcard sent to Selly Park on 31 August 1908. *Author's collection*

Trittiford Park. This postcard view was sent to Bristol on 3rd September 1931.    *Author's collection*

The River Cole in the area of Yardley Wood steel mill. This view is from a postcard sent to Solihull on September 17 1905.
                                                                                    *Author's collection*

A young lady poses for the camera by Windmill Farm at the end of Priory Road.

*Author's collection*

An auto train passes the nearly new station at Yardley Wood c1908-9.

*Author's collection*

# MEMORIES

## Memories of Adrian Cottages, High Street.

Viv Lawson (nee Fenton) remembers her childhood days living at No 5 Adrian Cottages.

The cottages were 16 terraced houses at a 90 degree angle from the High Street, so as you went up the long (and quite wide-maybe 10ft) entry next to Decorwalls you came to the side wall of No. 1 which had a beautiful Victorian logo (in terracotta or brick?) near the roof apex which just said 'Adrian Cottages 1895'. To the left hand side a wide path went round and up past the front gardens and to the right there was a really narrow alleyway to the back yards. I seem to remember that the writing on the wall of No 1 was raised and I think it was terracotta coloured, and yes, the top of it was about level with the gutters so you had to crane your neck right back to look up at it.

The houses were quite small but had three floors. On the ground floor the front door led straight into the front room, a door led into the living room and from the other side of that another one straight on into the teeny kitchen. The stairs led up from the left side of the living room and curved at the bottom and then again at the top where the landing was in the middle of the house and two first floor bedrooms led off on either side. The stairs carried on up and did a u-turn up to the L-shaped attic bedroom which had a large window in the roof looking out of the front, this was my bedroom. The view from the attic was great, it looked out over the garages and then to the back of the shops in Poplar Road. My granddad had a motorbike and sidecar (see opposite). He rented a garage which I could see from the attic and when he worked on Saturday mornings I used to hang out of the window waiting for him to come home then when I saw him I'd run down and tell Nan who would get his lunch on the table for him! There were two rows of garages and an actual garage with pumps up the driveway next to our entry (which was bang opposite the Baptist church and where the entry to the supermarket car park is now).

There were no bathrooms in the cottages, we had a zinc bath which was kept in the back yard and which came in on Sunday night for us all to bath in. I was lucky – being the smallest I always got to go in first! The bath wasn't that big but it filled the kitchen. When I was really small and the weather was just too cold to get the bath in, Nan used to take me to Institute Road baths and we would hire

*Opposite top:* Marjorie Ellen Jordan with grandson in pram in 1952. The petrol pumps are visible over the wall with the Baptist Chapel prominent on the other side of the High Street. The side wall of Decorwalls is seen on the left. *courtesy Viv Lawson*

*Opposite bottom:* Leslie John Jordan with motor cycle and side car outside his garage next to Adrian Cottages. The houses in Poplar Avenue can be seen in the background. *courtesy Viv Lawson*

a bathroom there. I remember it being all dark wood and big white enamel baths and it was real luxury to us being so warm. The cottages were cold in the winter – I remember scraping the ice off the inside of the attic window in the mornings to see what the weather was doing. We had a coal fire in the living room and it was a real treat to have potatoes baked in the ashes on a cold night! There was a fireplace in the front room too but that was only ever lit at Christmas.

At the back of the houses we all had private fenced back yards with an outside toilet next to the kitchen and a coal house. We were overlooked at the back by the houses in Hoddesdon Place so all our windows had net curtains. I thought we were much 'posher' than they were, as we had our own loo – all their toilets were in blocks at either end of the row and they had to share one toilet between two houses! As you went up our back alley there was a wall on the right hand side about four feet high, with wood and wire palings on top to separate the houses as Hoddesdon Place was on slightly higher ground than us. I remember when I was really young being bitten by red ants who

had nested in the wall outside our back gate.

There were long gardens behind the shops on the High Street over the wall in Hoddesdon Place. No one looked after them and us kids used to make dens out of the stuff people dumped there (mattresses, old doors, cardboard boxes etc). I remember playing with big false pies and models of meat joints at the back of Barrs, the Pork Butchers shop, which they threw out! My granddad used to send me to Barrs on Saturdays when they boiled pigs trotters and hocks and I would get a boiling hot one for his lunch. He used to get real pork scratchings and black and white pudding from there, which he shared with me (a real treat!)

I remember the houses in Hoddesdon Place being empty for a while and we had a plague of rats that moved in after the people moved out! Hoddesdon Place was demolished a couple of years before we moved out.

In the building at the very back of Decorwalls there were big wooden doors (facing the end wall of the Cottages) that were never opened. There was a printing press in there and when I was small you

Jean Fenton and her son, Steve in their Triumph Herald in front of the garage c1970. Motor mechanics still did repairs at this time but the petrol pumps had now disappeared. Adrian Cottages are seen to the right.

*courtesy Viv Lawson*

could hear it going but I've no idea who worked there or what they printed.

I've been thinking about when we used to make a Guy for bonfire night and stand at the bottom of the entry by the metal pole and ask for pennies. As soon as we had enough for a firework, one of us would run down to Darlastons and buy one. We had some good bonfires in our front garden and all the neighbours would join in and bring baked potatoes, sausages and rolls and all the kids ran round with sparklers (you wouldn't be allowed these days, parents are too scared with health & safety etc). How times have changed, eh?!

I went to King's Heath infants and junior school in Institute Road. I used to love swimming and when I got my free pass from school I used to go straight from the school gate, over the road to the baths pretty well every night.

## More memories of Adrian Cottages

John and Elizabeth Mushing are seen below outside their home at 5 Adrian Cottages in the early 1920s. The alleyway leading to Adrian Cottages is now the entrance from High Street to the supermarket car park. Brian Walsh, whose mother and grandparents lived at no. 4 relates the following "The cottages were actually two-storey terraced houses with an attic. The straight row of sixteen cottages were served by a blue brick path leading to the wooded back gates and a slightly wider path leading to the front gates. Despite the post at the entrance from the High Street it seems that the milkman's cart and other deliveries were able to access the wider front path to the front of the cottages. Each front garden was surrounded by iron railings and there was an iron gate between

*courtesy Joan Andrews*

every two cottages. When you first reached the cottages along the path from the High Street there was an iron railing fence surrounding the side of the first cottage and a gas lamp – a place that Mom and her friends congregated, much to the annoyance of their neighbours! The scullery had one of those shallow, brown crock sinks and a copper boiler.

Access to the yard, outside toilet and coalhouse was gained via the back door from the scullery. The cottage had gas lighting only and a rent collector called every week." Adrian Cottages were built in 1895 and survived until the mid to late 1970s being demolished after the neighbouring Hoddesdon Place disappeared during re-development of the site.

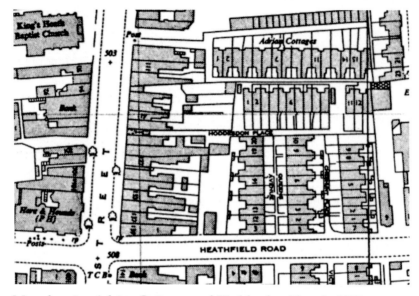

Map showing Adrian Cottages and Hoddesdon Place in 1955.

*Crown copyright reserved*

## Memories of Bob Chedgzoy

There used to be a dance hall in York Road, next to the Hare & Hounds called the Ritz. The site was also a snooker hall and previously part of the Ideal Cinema which fronted onto the High Street. Bob Chedgzoy, formerly of Fairfield Road remembers an historic occasion when the Beatles came to King's Heath. This is his account of that day.

"It was in the sixties just after their first No. 1 Hit. They were performing at the dance hall in York Road next door to the pub, the dance hall did not have a dressing room so the Beatles had to use the home of Bert Holmer (a friend of my father) located behind the dance hall to change in. That particular evening I had just returned from doing a job in my dad's works van, on my return I parked on the opposite side of York Road and went to the gents' only room in the Hare & Hounds to meet him. I had noticed on my arrival that a large crowd of young girls had gathered outside the dance hall

but did not think much of it at the time. My Dad was sat with Bert and four young lads who I did not know, they were wearing collarless blue blazers with some sort of badge. During the interval Bert took them back into his house for a pint. This is about my only claim to fame!"

The following from 'The Complete Beatles Chronicle' by Mark Lewisohn confirms Bob's Memories of the event.

"On Friday 11th January 1963 the Beatles made the hazardous afternoon journey south from Liverpool to Old Hill, blizzards ensured that they were unable to drive the 11 miles from there to King's Heath to fulfil the second part of a double booking in the Midlands. It was the coldest night in the area for seven years.
However, on Friday 15th February 1963 the Beatles appeared at the Ritz to fulfill the re-arranged

postponed booking. The situation was ideal for the Ritz promoters who presented the group now featuring in the top three of the singles chart at the same cost as when they were a comparatively unknown act."

The Rolling Stones also appeared at the Ritz in the 1960s and one wonders if the modern King's Heath could attract up and coming stars or do we lack a suitable venue like the Ritz?

Bob Chedgzoy also has some Fairfield Road history.

"I was told the houses in Fairfield Road cost £64.00 each to build, not surprising since they had no foundations or damp course! As dad and I discovered when we dug down to do some remedial work. I can remember in the 40s my parents were paying 3/4d a week rent. There were 30 terraced houses originally with three bedrooms, a front parlour, a living room with a range for cooking, a scullery with coal fired wash boiler and an outside toilet and coal house. The houses were gas lit and the water supply was a cold tap in the scullery. We lived at No. 22, my parents moved in on their marriage in 1932, they were both working at Regent Woodcraft at the rear of High Street at that time and I can only assume that is why they moved to King's Heath since they both came from Sparkbrook."

Bob has added the following to the news item of 10th November 1933 reported in the first book regarding the fire at Regent Woodworking Co. at the rear of Coopers:

'My Mum, Dad, Jane Turner (my aunt, later Jane Chedgzoy) and Mrs Frost were all employed there at that time. Mum was a French polisher and Dad was a wood machinist. It was always thought the fire was deliberate and started by means of placing a candle in a celluloid saucer and surrounding it with wood shavings, a simple but effective time delay fuse which would leave no trace. The Regent as it was known made "antique" furniture which Mum distressed by hitting it with a brick contained in a sock. Then she French polished it and dulled the now dry polish by rubbing it with the back of the sandpaper'.

Bob also has the following tale to tell about the bomb damaged houses in Wheelers Lane shown on page 47 of the first book.

"One of the houses belonged to Mrs. Barr of the High Street butchers. Dad knew her and did work for her. The story goes that when the bomb went off she was just entering the under stairs pantry with a freshly made custard pie. She suffered a face full of custard pie but was otherwise unhurt. This probably saved her life!"

The Regent Woodcraft Company workforce take a break from work in the yard behind Coopers greengrocers' shop 1925/6. Evelyn Genoe, later Mrs. Chedgzoy is at the left on the front row and Leslie Chedgzoy, Bob's father can be seen in the background to the left of the lady in the back row.
*courtesy Bob Chedgzoy*

# NEWS ITEMS

More interesting articles from the local journals and newspapers.

### September 1894.   Local barber in court.

Mr. William Ganniicliffe, hairdresser, of High Street, King's Heath, has found to his cost that combining the occupation of betting with his legitimate occupation does not pay. There may not be a fortune in his honourable calling of barber, but the trap he fell into has resulted in his banking account being considerably reduced. Mr. Ganniicliffe's recent appearance before the administrators of the law at King's Heath must have fully convinced that gentleman that he had better stick to his scissors and razor manipulations. The mystery, however, is how Mr. Gunniicliffe had the nerve to open a betting depot, with Police Superintendent Wasley of all men, in close proximity. If the tradesmen of King's Heath would only support the unfortunate barber more liberally, there will be no necessity for him to seek to increase his income by illegal means. "Out of evil may come good!"

### Spinsters' Ball.

One of the most interesting and enjoyable events last month, was the Spinsters' Ball, held at the King's Heath Institute on the 16th. There was a very large attendance—nearly 200. Mr. J. Horton officiated as M. C., and very admirably did he carry out his duties. The "belles", judging by those present at the dance, certainly could hold their own for beauty. As for the dresses of the ladies, it goes without saying these were varied and in great taste. Mr. Gregory's band supplied the music.

### August 1895.   High Street paving

The partial paving of the High Street of King's Heath has now been accomplished, but there is some dissatisfaction—more especially among the tradesmen—on account of the authorities only paving six feet. It is a well known and recognised fact however, that no authority is called upon to lay more than that number of feet of paving; indeed, it is questionable whether the County Council are under any legal obligation to do any paving, the footpaths in many districts being looked upon as coming under the province of the local governing body.

### October 1895.   Late running trains.

I have received several letters, and heard no end of grumbles—justifiable grumbles, too—with regard to the lateness of the trains during the last month running from King's Heath to town, especially the morning trains. Many times they have been half-an-hour late. What is the cause of it all? We have been passably free from this nuisance for the past years or so, and now, just on the eve of a great reformation, we are troubled worse than ever. Is this in fulfilment of the axiom that "The darkest hour is always before the dawn," or are the Midland Railway Company endeavouring by these means to emphasise the advantages that will result from the extensive alterations that are being carried out, and will enable us to run in double quick-time? In any case they are responsible for the utterance of most unbecoming language and a great amount of inconvenience to their patrons.

## January 1896.   Poor street lighting.

Residents of King's Heath have unfortunately, many good causes for complaints to the governing body of that "ilk." Their number may be composed of the lights of genius in the district, but they have some very dark spots in the neighbourhood. Ashfield Avenue is one of them, and should certainly receive immediate attention. There is no light whatever in the two roads forming the thoroughfare, except that supplied by the several residences. It has become unsafe for unprotected females to pass that way after dark, several having already been molested. The police would do well to pay a little more attention to this locality, and put a stop to many evils.

## April 1896.   The decline of the King's Heath Brewery.

The old gives way to the new. No sooner is the Grange Estate at King's Heath opened up then the good old firm, Frederick Everitt & Co., the King's Heath Brewery, falls into the hands of a big syndicate. How different things are now-a-days. As in America, so in England—everything is now being done on a big scale. The Everitt family has always been popular in this neighbourhood, and we shall miss their personal associations still more.

## September 1896.  Postal delivery petition.

A petition is being numerously signed praying the postal authorities to extend the facilities of delivery of letters in the King's Heath district. At present there is no Sunday delivery, and those expecting letters have to send to the local post office for them at an early hour. This state of affairs ought not, and cannot, remain much longer in so important and growing a district.

## November 1896.  The filthy state of King's Heath Railway Station.

There has been a good deal of correspondence going on lately in the columns of the dailies respecting the filthy state of King's Heath Railway Station. At one period of railway history the Midland Railway

Company were considered the pioneers of the times. To this great and enterprising company the public are very greatly indebted—for one thing especially, the initiation of the third class by all trains. Now that their attention has been drawn to the state of King's Heath Station, and the approaches to it, we may expect the Midland Railway Company to carry out the needed improvements.

By the way, this reminds me of the police court proceedings the other day at King's Heath when several young "lidies" out Selly Oak way were charged with defrauding the Midland Railway Company by riding first-class with third class tickets. The bench imposed a fine of 2s. 6d. And costs on four of them, while the fifth, whose Christian name was Prudence, appears to have been a little more prudent than her companions, for she was fined 1s. only and costs. If the authorities at Five Ways station would look as sharply after the passengers by the early afternoon trains to New Street they would be conferring a favour on the first-class passengers from New Street to Moseley and King's Heath !

## December 1897.  Improved Tram Service.

There is to be an improvement in the Moseley and King's Heath tram services. At a recent meeting of the King's Norton District Council the Highways and Bridges Committee reported that they had under consideration an application from the City of Birmingham Tramways Company for consent to alter certain lines with the object of providing a five-minute service on the Moseley and King's Heath routes, and they recommended that permission should be given in cases where it could be shown that the width of the road was sufficient to allow double sets of rails without endangering vehicular and passenger traffic. The committee were negotiating for a strip of land at Welch's Hill, Moseley, for the purpose of widening the road at that dangerous part. The report was adopted.

## February 1898.  King's Heath passenger caught defrauding the railway company.

It is strange how some people will run the risk of getting into trouble, public exposure and disgrace, in order to "do" a railway company. Here's a case in point. Alfred Abbett Pinkney, of Clarence Road, was summoned at the King's Heath Police Court last month for travelling on the Midland Railway without a ticket, and with intent to avoid payment of his fare.

In the course of the evidence for the prosecution, it was stated that the defendant was seen by one of the ticket collectors at King's Heath to alight from a first-class compartment. On being asked by the collector for his fare, the defendant handed a penny, saying that he had a season ticket from Birmingham to Moseley. He was then requested to show his ticket, whereupon he produced a third-class season ticket. Upon being told by the collector that he had seen him alight from a first-class carriage, he took his name and address. Defendant snatched at the paper, saying, "If you are going to make any bother I will pay."

Sharp practice is a very hard trait in any person. Mr. Pinkney must have regretted his action in the matter, in order to "do" the railway company. His name has gone into print, and his sharp practice has consequently been publicly exposed in the papers. The Justices, Mr. Playfair and Sir J. C. Holder, Bart., fined Pinkney five shillings and costs.

I understand that other people are guilty of "doing" the railway company by travelling from New Street out this way first-class with a third-class ticket. In some cases the railway authorities have been communicated with, and a watch has been put on the passengers' movements. People who do this thing deliberately, and with intent to defraud, are deserving of public exposure in the police courts and in the papers.

But I have not done. There is another class of the travelling public who do not scruple to "pinch" anything that comes their way. A Moseley gentleman was telling me the other day that he left his umbrella in the rack of a first-class compartment. Just as the train started for King's Heath he thought of it, but it was too late. From that day to this he has seen nothing of his umbrella. One would hardly expect to find a first-class passenger bemean himself in this manner. Yet, strange to say, there are those who are proud to "sneak" anything that comes in their way, whenever they can get an opportunity, and they consider themselves very clever.

## August 1898. The R. F. F. Dairy opens a branch in King's Heath.

King's Heath residents—after a long-felt want—have now the opportunity afforded them of buying at their own doors milk, eggs, and butter, "fresh from the farm daily." The R. F. F. Dairy have opened a branch opposite King's Heath Station—Railway Station, I mean—where everything sold will be of the very best. The R. F. F. Are making a speciality of poultry—farm fed—none of your wretched half-starved Irish importation, consisting of nothing but skin and bones, and tough as leather! The poultry at the newly-opened establishment, opposite King's Heath Railway Station, will be found to be plump and tender and moderate in price. Orders will be delivered daily. Tea and refreshments can be obtained and parties catered for.

## January 1899. Boy saved from serious injury in tram car incident.

No little consternation was caused on a Moseley tram car one day last month, when a boy, Leslie Goold by name, and a son of Mr. Lewis Goold, a well-known and popular King's Heath resident, was saved from a severe if not fatal accident by fellow schoolmate – Tom Carpenter, of 10, Ashfield Road, King's Heath. It appears that the sliding door at the far end of the car slipped back when Leslie went to sit down, with the result that the little fellow pitched head-first, and but for the celerity of Tom Carpenter, who seized hold of his foot, the result would unquestionably have been serious. Master Carpenter is a bright and well mannered boy, and is a great credit to Tindal Street Board School.

Mr. & Mrs. Goold have shown their appreciation of Master Carpenter's conduct by presenting him with a beautiful stamp album inscribed with the following : — "To Tom Carpenter with Mr. & >Mrs. Goold's best wishes and a slight indication of their appreciation of his presence of mind in saving their son Leslie from what otherwise might have been a fatal accident in the tram. December 1898."

## January 1901. Planned new public building.

What a great place King's Heath is becoming to be sure. Only a few years ago it was a village "near" Birmingham, but today it is of a size and has a population which might well be the envy of many towns with well known names. The latest phase of its development is a scheme for erecting a public building in the High Street between the Bank and the Baptist Chapel, which will serve as a Masonic Hall, and Assembly Room, and as Private Club Rooms. There is certainly a need at King's Heath of a social club after the style of the institution at Moseley, and I will have no doubt that the proposal to form such a club in King's Heath will meet with hearty and general support. The work is proceeding at a rapid rate. The plans of the new building have been prepared, and now Christmas is over the work of construction will begin.

## May 1901. Economy carriages for the Midland Railway Company.

The Midland Railway Company have gone and done it this time! The nobility and gentry of Moseley and King's Heath—those who travel first-class to town and back—are in arms owing to the arrangements of the new carriages. Whereas formerly there was accommodation for three aside, the Midland, by studying economy, which is now the order of the day, have done away with the arm-rests, and so not only save the cost of these but in consequence there is room for five persons on each side. As a result of all this manipulation fewer carriages are required and the overlapping of the platform at each end is avoided. For myself I am quite content to travel with the Moseley and King's Heath plebeians whose company, in more ways than one, is quite as good as that of many of the first-class season ticket holders, especially when some of these gentlemen are undischarged bankrupts!

## June 1901. Another King's Heath Grievance.

Someone has discovered that the depopulation of King's Heath is not entirely due to the outbreaks of diphtheria and scarlet fever. It is to be accounted for in a measure by the increased popularity of Brandwood End Cemetery as a last resting place.

The number of funerals increase; and, of course, most of them have of necessity to pass along the Alcester Road, with dismal procession of black coaches which, especially on Sundays, passes before their windows, and it is stated that it has had a distinct effect in sending people away from the district.

## The King's Heath Horse Show.

The King's Heath Horse Show is becoming a much more important event than we ever intended when it was first instituted. In the first year it boasted of only a baker's dozen of exhibits; in the following year it had 60; this year there were 217, of which no fewer than 154 were in the open classes. The substantial prize money—about £150 in all—attracted horse owners from Tamworth, Macclesfield, Derby, Cheltenham, and other parts of the country, and several winners at the Royal and other shows were exhibited. Altogether the exhibits, in number and quantity, and the attendance were most encouraging, and an exultant strain ran through the speeches at the luncheon, held in one of the tents on the ground in Priory Park, where the show was opened on Whit Monday. Mr. J. H. Cartland, the president, was unable to attend, but his place was capably filled by Mr. W. H. Parton, who made mention that over a hundred pounds had been received that year in subscriptions, as against a total income of only £30 in the previous year. The show is evidently booming along in a manner that must be specially gratifying to those officials who engineered it through its early difficulties.

## December 1915. Foundation Stone Laying Ceremony.

The foundation stone of the new Church Mission Room to be erected at Hazelwell, was laid on Saturday, 6th December by Miss Cartland. Among those present at the ceremony were Major Howard Cartland (the donor of the site) and other local dignitaries. After a short service held in All Saints' Church, a procession of choristers, clergy, various church workers, and representatives of parochial organisations proceeded to the site. Miss Bishop, daughter of the building contractor, Mr. W. Bishop, presented Miss Cartland with a handsome silver trowel, and Miss Dawson presented the spirit level and mallet. At the conclusion of the ceremony the procession re-formed and returned to the parish church.

### July 1927. New Park for King's Heath.
On the 11th ult., the Lord Mayor of Birmingham (Alderman A. H. James, C. B. E., J. P.) opened the park, which is to form one of the chief amenities of Holly Bank Village, an estate of 105 acres, lying between the Tramway Stadium and Wheelers Lane, with its main frontage in Haunch Lane.

### January 1932. Boys' Brigade Anniversary.
The sixth Birmingham Company of the Boys' Brigade celebrated their semi jubilee during last month at King's Heath Baptist Church School. The evening was opened by the chaplain, the Rev. W. J. Smallbone, and during the evening the president of the Birmingham Battalion (Mr. D. L. Finnemore) came. Those also present included Rev. J. G. Collett (first chaplain), Mr. Harrison (former lieutenant and once major of the Birmingham Battalion Boys' Life Brigade), Mrs. Thrussell, Messrs. Amplett, H. D. Clemments, W. J. Molineaux, S. G. W. Swift. The event was under the control of Captain A. T. Coltman.

The entertainment included a performance by the Company Concert Party and a B. B. Sketch, with fine staging and lighting effects.

### 31st March 1933. L.M.S. plans holiday specials from King's Heath.
Meeting Mr. Varty, the popular King's Heath station master, my thoughts sped rapidly to long stretches of golden sands, to majestic mountains, to purple moors, for he discoursed of the splendid schemes the L.M.S. have in hand this year for the holiday maker. More of this anon, but here is something that all King's Heath folk should know. Do not forget that All Day, Half-Day, Week-end and holiday return tickets can all be obtained at King's Heath Station. There is no need whatever to go into town, and by obtaining tickets at King's Heath Station much delay is saved in collection of passengers' luggage. This is

worth remembering. Mr. Varty will give the utmost assistance and advice to all intending travellers.

Trips to the following places are suggested; Evesham, Alton Towers, Leek, The Peak District, Burton, Worcester, Malvern and Weston-Super-Mare.

### 7th April 1933. Hazelwell Station opens for the summer season.
I say, what do you think, Hazelwell Station is opening on Easter Sunday, April 16th, for the whole of the summer season, thus providing full facilities for the residents of Dad's Lane and the Pineapple Estate. This will be a boon, and by the way, for the humble 6d. there are return tickets to the Lickies on Wednesday, Saturday and Sunday afternoons from Hazelwell and all day Sunday from King's Heath. I can see the Lickies being crowded this Summer, with such a splendid opportunity being provided by the L. M. S., and I must say I think it is a jolly nice outing, for if anyone cannot find beauty and refreshment in wandering over the lovely hills in the sunshine, then they must be hard to please.

### 27th October 1933. New shops and houses for King's Heath.
I hear that the houses between Arnold Genders & Co. and Kathleen Royles will shortly be coming down, and some new and most attractive shops going up. King's Heath is certainly growing in importance as a shopping centre every week, and no sooner does one see the site cleared for new houses before they seem to be up and occupied. Building operations have been on at the corner of Beechwood Road, and in Taylor Road, also at the front of the Institution in Haunch Lane, and at Hollywood many new houses are in course of erection. The new part of Hazelhurst Road is nearing completion. I believe Mr. Edwards, of Messrs. John Edwards & Son, is responsible for the fine houses in this road. I for one am glad that local builders have put up the houses. Those erected and in course of erection in Wheeler's Lane have mostly been carried out by Messrs. John Phillips & Son, and Messrs. John A. Edwards & Son, and very fine specimens of the builders art they are indeed, look you!

**14th June 1935. Road collapses at King's Heath.**

An alarming subsidence of the road in Vicarage Road, King's Heath, might have had serious consequences.

The collapse took place on Monday in Vicarage Road, near the junction of Avenue Road, where a new sewer is being laid to a length of road some 15 or 16 feet long and about 7 feet wide. The trench at the junction of Avenue Road was filled in on Friday. On Monday, a petrol lorry had a wonderful escape. The lorry weighing about 17 tons missed the piece of road which has now collapsed and went on the right hand side.

Apparently traffic has been running on nothing more than a surface six inches thick, with for some distance, nothing underneath.

**13th March 1936. Billesley Proposed Secondary School.**

It is proposed to erect a secondary school at Billesley. The Education Committee reporting on the proposal, states that during an exhaustive review of the City's needs in respect of accommodation for post-primary education, it came to the conclusion that a school for 500 girls should be provided as near as possible to the existing boy's school at Moseley. Enquiries were accordingly made for a suitable site, but the committee found that, owing to the rapid housing developments, there was virtually no land available and the only way out of the difficulty appeared to be by arrangement with the Parks Committee. That committee agreed to transfer to the Education Committee about sixteen acres of land between Wheeler's Lane and Yardley Wood Road, with access from Brook Lane. In the opinion of the district valuer, the market value of the site is £6,000 and the committee recommends that, subject to the approval of the Board of Education and the Minister of Health, the land be transferred to the Education Committee on the conditions stated.

# Amendments to the first volume

**Page 22 (Bottom)**  Christopher Hodgetts is the proprietor and not the motor cyclist or pillion passenger.
*Information courtesy Margaret Harrison*

**Page 49**  Caption for 'Opposite top' photograph (Page 48). Date of making Hollybank Road was c1952. The proposed road was shown on earlier maps but obviously the Second World War intervened.

**Page 61**  Caption should read W. F. Barr.

**Page 90 (Top)**  The two trams were a special tour for the 'Light Railway Transport League'. Tram 830 was from the Pershore Road service and would not normally be seen on the Moseley Road run through King's Heath.
*Information courtesy Garth Tilt*

**Page 111 (bottom)**  Teacher with School leavers is Mr. Moses and not Mr. Flavell.
*Information courtesy Michael Flavell*

**Page 118**  In text, Aaron Payton was born in 1777 (Not 1877).
*Information courtesy D. J. Silsby*

**Page 139 (Bottom)**  Thanks to Mr. Stanley Overton this location is confirmed as Prince of Wales Lane and shows his family home where he was born in 1920.

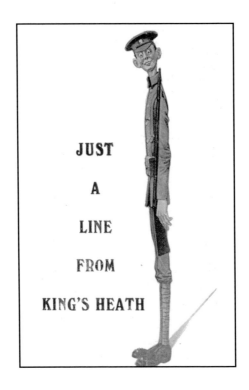

JUST

A

LINE

FROM

KING'S HEATH